Models ~for~ Writing

Chris Buckton

Anne Sanderson

Series editor: Leonie Bennett

Pupil's Book 6

Ginn

Symbols

 Group/individual work.

PCM A photocopy master is available to support differentiation.

Differentiation symbols.

1 Easy to complete.

2 All pupils complete activity. Activities are supported by a PCM for extra help.

3 More difficult activities.

Author Team: Chris Buckton
Anne Sanderson
Series Editor: Leonie Bennett

Ginn

Linacre House, Jordan Hill, Oxford, OX2 8DP
a division of Reed Educational and Professional Publishing Ltd
www.ginn.co.uk

Ginn is a registered trademark of Reed Educational and Professional
Publishing Ltd

ISBN 0602 296927

04 03 02
10 9 8 7 6 5 4

Designed and produced by Gecko Ltd, Bicester, Oxon
Cover designed by Gecko Ltd, Bicester, Oxon
Printed in Spain by Edelvives

Contents

1

RETELLING
Big Bad Wolf

The True Story of the Three Little Pigs

Jon Scieszka

Everybody knows the story of the Three
Little Pigs. *Or at least they think they do.*
But I'll let you in on a little secret. Nobody
knows the real story, because nobody has ever
5 *heard my side of the story.*

I'm the wolf. Alexander T Wolf.

first person

You can call me Al.

I don't know how this whole Big Bad
Wolf thing got started, but it's all wrong.
10 Maybe it's because of our diet.

Hey, it's not my fault that wolves eat
cute little animals like bunnies and
sheep and pigs. That's just the way
we are. If cheeseburgers were cute,
15 folks would probably think you
were Big and Bad, too.

chatty
tone –
addresses
reader

Way back in Once Upon a Time time,
I was making a birthday cake for my dear
old granny. I had a terrible sneezing cold.
20 I ran out of sugar.

So I went next door to ask if I could borrow
a cup of sugar.

Now the guy next door was a pig.

And he wasn't too bright, either.

25 He had built his house out of straw.

Can you believe it? I mean who in his right
mind would build a house out of straw? …

Reading

1 Work with a partner. Discuss how the wolf might tell the rest of the story. Why does he blow down the pigs' houses? How does he escape at the end?

2 Make notes to help you tell the story from memory.

3 Practise telling the story in the wolf's voice. Try to make him sound American!

Writing

Work with a partner. Do one of the following:

a Continue the story begun in shared writing. Write the next few paragraphs.

OR

PCM 2

b Write the rest of '**The True Story of the Three Little Pigs**' using your notes from yesterday to help you.

REMEMBER

Write in the first person.

Use a chatty style.

Think up some good excuses.

Keep to the original plot.

Extended Writing

Finish writing your story. You could write a short newspaper article and include it in the story.

2

NARRATION

Double Act

Jacqueline Wilson

EXTRACT ONE

We're twins. I'm Ruby. She's Garnet.

We're identical. There's very few people who can tell us apart.
Well, until we start talking. I tend to go on and on. Garnet is
much quieter.

5   *That's because I can't get a word in edgeways.*

We are exactly the same height and weight. I eat a bit more than
Garnet. I love sweets, and I like salty things too. I once ate
thirteen packets of crisps in one day. All salt-and-vinegar flavour.
I love lots of salt and vinegar on chips too. Chips are my special

10 weakness. I go munch munch munch gulp and they're gone. So ← conversational tone
then I have to snaffle some of Garnet's. She doesn't mind.

    Yes I do.

I don't get fatter because I charge around more. I hate sitting still.
Garnet will hunch up over a book for hours, but I get the fidgets.

'I don't *want* to be in showbiz. Look, you go if you want, but I'm not.'

'Oh ha ha, very helpful. How can I audition as a twin by myself, eh? Don't be such a dope. Now, where's the
5 book, we've got to get cracking. Which twin is which? I'll be the one that says the most. We'll work it so you don't have to say hardly anything, OK?'

'No, Ruby, please, *please*.' Garnet started scrabbling at me.

10 'We can't miss out on this, Garnet. It's our big chance. We've got to go for it.'

'But it says lively. I'm not a bit lively. I don't jump about like you, I just sort of flop in a corner. And I'm not outgoing. I'm as inwardbeing as you could possibly get.'

15 'You'll be OK. Just copy me.'

Why do I always have to copy Ruby?

different
points
of view

I can't act.

*I don't **want** to act.*

*I can't go to an audition in London! I can't say a lot of
20 stuff with everyone watching. Why won't Ruby understand? She won't listen to me. She's riffling through The Twins at St Clare's right this minute, trying to choose which bit we'll act out.*

Only I'm not going to act.

25 *I can't act. I can't act.*

Remember what Gran says? There's no such word as can't! Now stop scribbling and start spouting. We've got to be word-perfect by Monday!

Reading

1. Choose **one** twin. Write a paragraph about the audition from their point of view. Write in the first person. Try to write in a chatty style.

2. Write the other twin's version of the audition.

Writing

PCM 4

1. Make notes for your own story. Do not spend more than ten minutes on the planning. Look back at your homework notes to help you.

2. Start writing your first draft.

REMEMBER

Use the first person.

Use a chatty style.

Show different viewpoints.

Extended Writing

Continue with the first draft of your story. Read and revise it with a writing partner. Produce a final version.

NON-CHRONOLOGICAL REPORT

Eclipse of the Sun

On August 11th 1999, in south west England, darkness fell at 11.00 am. When this happened in ancient times, people thought the gods were angry with them and were terrified. Nowadays, we know it is an eclipse of the sun.

interesting introduction

A solar eclipse happens when the moon moves between the earth and the sun. Viewed from the earth, the moon masks out the sun. If the sun is only partly covered, it is a partial eclipse. If the sun is completely covered, it is a total eclipse.

describes what happens

The sun and moon appear to be almost the same size, when seen from the Earth. But the sun is about 400 times bigger in diameter than the moon, and 400 times further away from the earth.

Every day, the sun appears to rise in the east and set in the west and the moon appears to follow a very similar path – but at a slower pace. The sun and moon appear to move in this way because of the way the earth itself moves. Remember, the sun doesn't actually move at all.

Moon   Earth

Moon's shadow

Although the moon appears to shine, it has no light of its own. It reflects light from the sun. It is present in the sky for about half the daylight hours, but cannot always be seen. Every 29 days or so, at the time of the new moon, the sun seems to overtake the moon – usually passing above or below it. When it is directly behind the moon, there is a total eclipse of the sun.

impersonal
pronouns

Each point on the earth will be in a total eclipse once every 360 years. In the UK, this happened in the south west in 1999. Before that it was in the north east of England in 1927. The next total eclipse of the sun in the UK will occur in 2090. For most people it's a once-in-a-lifetime event!

Sources of information:

Total Eclipse of the Sun in Cornwall and South Devon, by Pam Hine, 1999, Yarner Press

http://umbra.nascom.nasa.gov/eclipse/990811/rp.html
(one of the main NASA Internet sites concerning the 1999 eclipse)

can the report quickly. Write down:

two things you already knew

the two most interesting facts

one amazing fact

pairs, decide on short headings for each paragraph.

st the key points (facts) given in paragraph 3 of the
port.

st the key points given in paragraphs 4 and 5.

Writing

1. Using **sheet 6** write down the title of your report and the paragraph headings from shared writing.

2. Look at the *What we know* list from shared writing. Which key points could you put in each paragraph? Note them down.

3. What other information do you want to put in your report? Begin to look in books or CD ROMs for answers to your questions. Make notes.

REMEMBER

The first paragraph is an introduction.

Use mostly the present tense.

Include description.

Check your facts.

Use impersonal pronouns, e.g. it, they, them.

Extended Writing

1. Finish researching your report. Plan and write your first draft.

2. Swap drafts with a partner. Check that the report includes impersonal pronouns, and is written mainly in the present tense.

3. Edit your work carefully, and produce a final, neat copy.

AUTOBIOGRAPHY

Food, Glorious Food

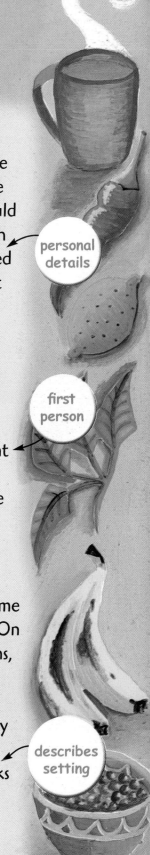

Coming to England

Food played a very important part in our lives. Marmie insisted that we had plenty of it and her cupboards were never empty. She insisted we all ate well so that we would grow up big and strong. Mind you, we didn't need much
5 encouragement – it was always a race to see who finished first or who ate the most food. Not a scrap was ever left on the plates. For breakfast we would have fresh home-baked bread, scrambled eggs or saltfish, fresh fruits and tea, which could mean anything from grated cocoa,
10 coffee or tea itself. After breakfast we had to line up to be given a dose of cod liver oil which was hideous. The fishy, oily liquid seemed to line the inside of the throat and stay there. It was one of the few things I didn't want to be first in line for and when it was my turn I used to
15 hold my nose and only the promise of a piece of orange would encourage me to take it. Marmie told us it was good for our bones and teeth, which was true but it didn't make it taste any better.

Sunday was a special day in Trinidad. It was the one time
20 of the week when we all got together. We ate lavishly. On the menu would be brown down chicken, rice, plantains, callaloo, sweet potatoes, cassavas, gungo peas and macaroni cheese pie. To drink we would have soursop juice or limeade made from fresh fruit and ice bought by
25 my mother from the ice truck which came round every day. Not many people had refrigerators so the big blocks of ice would be wrapped in a sackcloth and newspaper and would be kept in a big wooden tub.

Floella Benjamin

personal details

first person

describes setting

One Child's War

The thing I remember most about our Pat was the way he ate. He led the fashion in this. If we had porridge Pat would start from the outside, cutting away from the edge with his spoon, round and round till he

5 had a sugary island in the middle of a milky sea, which was the last to go. Cornflakes we all three crushed and crunched into the milk. It was quite an industry this, three spoons pounding and crunching until the crispy flakes were in a mush. Later, when Bridie came to stay,

10 we were told that the correct way to eat them was in the crispy state, but this was never such fun. One thing I was loath to copy, though it's likely I did for a while, was the mushing up into a marbled mound the greens and potatoes and the mince we had for dinner. This

15 was done with a fork. Not a mouthful would be eaten till the separate portions were mixed in together, then smoothed into a pie shaped mould with a knife. Sometimes it was a diamond shape or textured with a fork. We also drank gallons of hot sweet tea, which was

20 particularly marvellous after a chip butty – hot chips melting the butter and warming the bread with just a tang of vinegar and salt. Smashing! The hot tea would swill down the oiliness. My mother always complained of the way Pat swilled down the tea through mouthfuls

25 of food, but never of how we copied him. It was Joe, in fact, who invented the jelly butty – the trifle variety of jelly, between two slices of bread!

Food was fun, despite the war restrictions and we all ate mountains of it.

Victoria Massey

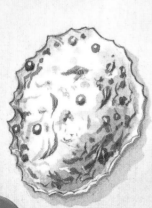

humour

Reading

1 Do you mess about with food or have a special way of eating some foods? Do you lick the chocolate off the outside of biscuits first? Do you make shapes or pies with mashed potato? Write a sentence describing how you eat one particular food.

2 Which foods would you prefer to eat – Floella's or Victoria's? Explain why.

Writing

Using your homework notes, write an autobiographical account of a meal you remember eating. If it was good, make it mouth-watering!
If it was bad, make sure we know why.

REMEMBER

Chatty style.

Scrummy details – look, smell, taste.

Describe your feelings.

Extended Writing

Read the first draft of your account to a partner. Does it have the required effect? Could you improve it by adding or cutting sections? Make any improvements and write your final version.

5

PERSONIFICATION

I Met At Eve

I met at eve the Prince of Sleep,
His was a still and lovely face.
He wandered through a valley steep,
  Lovely in a lonely place.

His garb was grey of lavender,
About his brows a poppy-wreath
Burned like dim coals, and everywhere
  The air was sweeter for his breath.

His twilight feet no sandals wore,
His eyes shone faint in their own flame,
Fair moths that gloomed his steps before
  Seemed letters of his lovely name.

His house is in the mountain ways,
A phantom house of misty walls,
Whose golden flocks at evening graze,
　　And 'witch the moon with muffled calls.

Upwelling from his shadowy springs
Sweet waters shake a trembling sound,
There flit the hoot-owl's silent wings,
　　There hath his web the silkworm wound.

Dark in his pools clear visions lurk,
And rosy, as with morning buds,
Along his dales of broom and birk
　　Dreams haunt his solitary woods.

I met at eve the Prince of Sleep,
His was a still and lovely face.
He wandered through a valley steep,
　　Lovely in a lonely place.

Walter de la Mare

Reading

1 Read the phrases on **sheet 9**. Underline any examples of alliteration. On the outline provided, draw details of what the Prince of Sleep might look like.

2 With a partner, read verses 5 and 6 of the poem on **sheet 10**.

a Underline 'poetic' words and phrases. Look up the meanings of any words you are not sure about. Write down some 'everyday' alternatives. Use a thesaurus to help you.

b Mark examples of alliteration and onomatopoeia.

c Mark examples of 'poetic' word order.

Writing

PCM 12

1 Compose your own poem about Night. Do not try to make it rhyme. Concentrate on describing the kind of person that Night might be.

2 Read your first draft to your partner. Can they suggest any improvements?

REMEMBER

Personification means talking about an abstract idea as if it were a person.

Make every detail fit the mood.

Extended Writing

Revise your poem and write a final draft to read aloud in a future lesson or assembly.

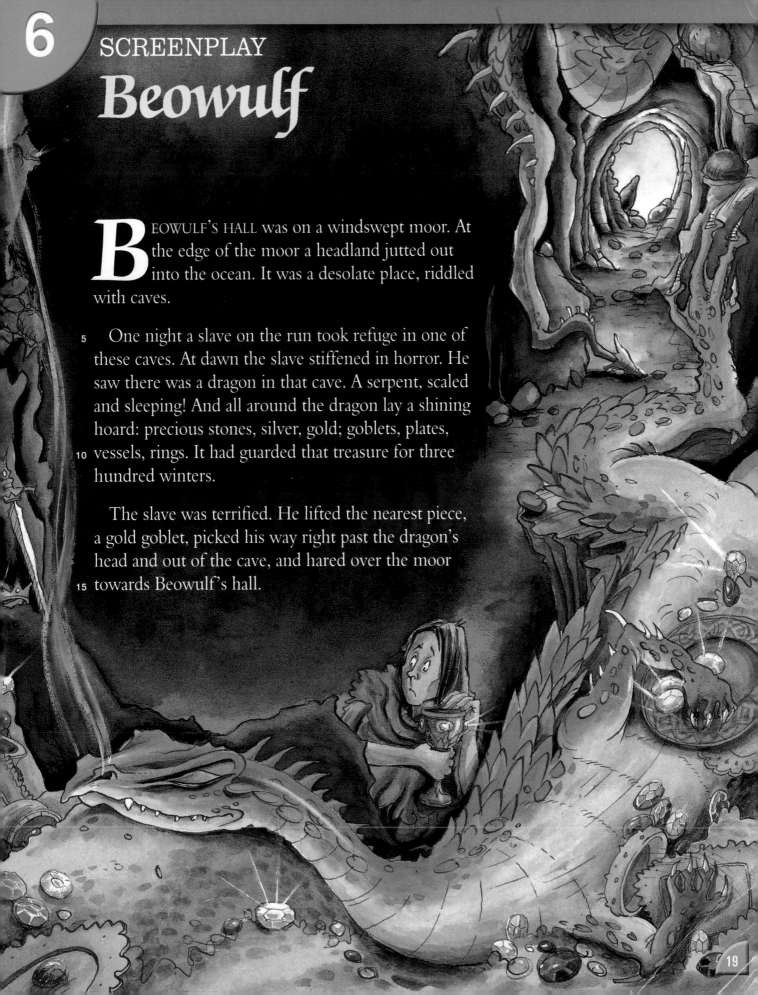

6

SCREENPLAY
Beowulf

BEOWULF'S HALL was on a windswept moor. At the edge of the moor a headland jutted out into the ocean. It was a desolate place, riddled with caves.

5   One night a slave on the run took refuge in one of these caves. At dawn the slave stiffened in horror. He saw there was a dragon in that cave. A serpent, scaled and sleeping! And all around the dragon lay a shining hoard: precious stones, silver, gold; goblets, plates,
10 vessels, rings. It had guarded that treasure for three hundred winters.

The slave was terrified. He lifted the nearest piece, a gold goblet, picked his way right past the dragon's head and out of the cave, and hared over the moor
15 towards Beowulf's hall.

When the dragon woke from its long sleep, it realised at once that its hoard had been robbed: it snorted and a twisting flame-torque leaped out of its mouth. The dragon took revenge. As soon as it was dark it swooped on the Geats and
20 girdled their stronghold with fire.

When day dawned once more, Beowulf and his companions saw the terrible damage and destruction – buildings gutted or collapsed, exposed to the elements; charred gables and beams; smouldering heaps of ash. All the land round about had been
25 laid waste; it looked like fields of stubble fired after harvesting.

Beowulf called the warrior Geats to a meeting.

A crowd of pale faces; a current of voices; a counting of heads.

'Never,' said Beowulf, 'has there been an
30 enemy such as this. But if we wait, it will be worse: this dragon will pay us a second visit. There's only one way to put an end to this threat, and only one man who can do it.'

Retold by *Kevin Crossley-Holland*

Reading

PCM 13

1. Summarise the second and third paragraphs in one sentence each. Use as few words as possible.

PCM 13

2. Imagine you are making a film of **Beowulf**. Read through the extract carefully. Make a list of all the events you want to show in your film. Remember that in a film you can show events that aren't described in the text.

Writing

PCM 15

1. Work with a partner. Using **sheet 14** plan a screenplay for the first three scenes of **Beowulf**. Use the notes from shared writing to help you .

2. Think about what action, dialogue and sound effects you will include.

3. Work out each camera shot. Make brief notes for each shot.

Extended Writing

Write your screenplay. Design more detailed storyboards for each scene.

REMEMBER

Film terms

close-up

middle distance

long shot

zoom in/out

tilt up/down

pan across

fade in/out

sound effects

action

dialogue

In the News

SUNDAY 22ND MARCH 1998

Record men fall to earth with a bump

by Andrew Buncombe
in Egypt

gives facts →

After **21 days** and **29,000** miles in the air, there were two things balloonist Brian Jones wanted to do when he landed in the Egyptian desert: to urinate without having to use a plastic bottle and to wash his hair. Jones did both in that order.

Jones and his co-pilot, Bertrand Piccard, were delighted that they had circumnavigated the globe by balloon. 'The best bit ... has to be the finishing line,' said Jones, a 51-year-old grandfather from Wiltshire. 'It's a surreal feeling.'

The pair touched down at 05.52 GMT yesterday; their adventure having ended in Egypt's Western Desert. After two failed attempts at landing, the pair brought down the 170ft tall balloon third time lucky. 'The eagle has landed,' Jones announced.

Brian Jones and Bertrand Piccard celebrate their record-breaking journey

human interest

The Breitling Orbiter balloon

The pair then waited for eight hours until they were recovered by an Egyptian Air Force helicopter.

'We were in another world. It was a little piece of paradise.'

In Cairo, last night, the two adventurers told how each had helped the other: 'We were in another world. It was a little piece of paradise,' said Piccard, 41. Jones added, 'For 21 days, we didn't have a single cross word, not even a slight criticism.'

They became the first balloonists to circumnavigate the world non-stop – 17 other attempts, including two by Mr Piccard, having failed – shortly before 10.00 GMT on Saturday.

Piccard said he was honoured to have achieved one of the last few challenges left to adventurers. Jones said he would have to think very hard before accepting another challenge. What would he do next? 'Ask me later,' he said.

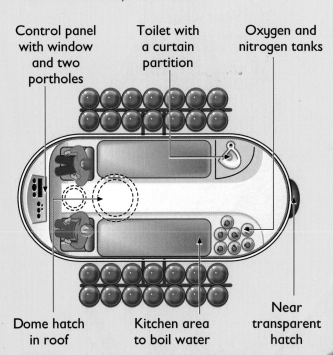

Control panel with window and two portholes — Toilet with a curtain partition — Oxygen and nitrogen tanks — Dome hatch in roof — Kitchen area to boil water — Near transparent hatch

Reading

1 Read the rest of the article, then write down three questions which the journalist might have asked the balloonists before writing his report.

2 Look at the first paragraph. Find two amazing facts and two amusing facts.

3 Scan the report to help you finish these sentences.

a

An example of Piccard's direct speech is, '................
....,'

b

Jones is reported to have said that ....
....

Writing

Write your own newspaper article about **Beowulf**.

1 Decide on a 'punchy' headline for the article.

2 Write an interesting first paragraph, which will make the reader want to read on.

3 Using the paragraph headings from shared writing, plan what you will include in the other paragraphs.

PCM
17

REMEMBER

Include some facts.

Include opinions or 'eye witness' accounts.

Make your first sentence grab the readers' interest.

Extended Writing

1 Complete a first draft of your article. Ask a partner to read it and comment on journalistic features, spellings and punctuation.

2 Design a layout for the article. Use columns. Plan the headline, size of lettering and typeface. Decide what space you need for pictures.

3 Use a word processor to complete a final draft, and ask a partner to proof-read it before publishing.

SCHOOL REPORT
Summing Up

Westward County Primary School

Record of Achievement for

Jane Johnson

Class 3	Year 5	Key Stage 2	Class Teacher Mrs Sharp
Date of entry 6-9-94			Languages spoken other than English /
Date of birth 5-12-89			
Total sessions 344	Absences 5		Unauthorised absences 0
This record is based on the teacher's assessments of progress			✓
This record is based on teacher assessments and national curriculum standard assessment task results			

General progress

Teacher's comments on personal and social development: in working with others, independence and maturity, helpfulness and reliability and reasons for significant absences. Special achievements and needs are included.

English

Jane's work in English is slowly improving. She reads aloud expressively and her reading age has gone up. However, she does not always understand what she has read, particularly in non-fiction texts. Consequently she finds answering questions difficult and tends not to join in class discussion.

Her writing, although clear, is often barely punctuated and is painfully slow. To manage real improvement here she needs to speed up next year. Her spelling is reasonable and she is beginning to adopt strategies to tackle unknown words.

Mathematics

Jane moves in 'fits and starts' in mathematics. She can add and subtract competently and has recently become proficient in multiplying. She needs to learn her tables.

When the sums are straightforward Jane copes well, but she becomes very worried when the problems, however simple, are wrapped up in words. She seems to lack the confidence to unravel them.

She knows her shapes and can measure and weigh, and can draw bar graphs.

Science

Jane seems interested in science and can carry out investigations if they are carefully directed. She works well as part of a group. She is not very forthcoming in talking about her work and often finds it difficult to write about her findings.

I think that as her knowledge and confidence grows, however, this will improve.

Reading

1 Complete the summary of Jane's progress on **sheet 18**. Look back at her report to help you.

2 a In rough, draft a summary of not more than 50 words to describe Jane's general progress. Look back at her report to help you.

b Read your summary to a partner and make any improvements. Keep your sentences short.

c Copy it in your best handwriting in the box on **sheet 19**.

Writing

1 Using the blank school report on **sheet 20,** write your own school report.

Fill in the details at the top. Decide which subjects you are going to write about. Write one subject in each box.

2 In rough, begin to draft each part of the report. Do not forget to include a summary of general progress.

3 Read your draft to your partner and make any improvements.

4 Fill in the report.

REMEMBER

Use

short sentences

clear punctuation

facts not opinions

present tense

Extended Writing

Finish the final draft of your report.

BIOGRAPHY

Harriet Tubman
Freedom fighter

gives facts

Harriet Tubman was born in 1820 in the American South, where many slaves worked on large farms and plantations. She and her family were owned 5 by a rich farmer, and lived in a small shack, with no furniture and only a bare, dirt floor to sleep on.

Harriet was only three years old when she was first put to work carrying 10 messages. By the age of nine she was cleaning and babysitting for her master and other rich families who lived nearby. Some of these people were cruel to her, but she dared not 15 complain in case she was sold and separated from her family.

past tense

At night, Harriet loved to listen to the adult slaves talking about freedom, and she vowed that 20 one day she would be free. In 1849 she heard a rumour that her master was going to sell some of his slaves, so she decided to escape.

25 She headed North on a long and dangerous journey on the 'underground railway'. This was not a real railway, but a special 30 route for escaped slaves

set up by people who believed slavery was wrong. The escaping slaves were known as 'passengers' and hid in safe houses called 'stations'. The people who organised the
35 railway and helped the slaves were called 'conductors'.

In the north of America there was no slavery, and when Harriet finally reached Pennsylvania she was free. However, she
40 couldn't stop thinking about her family, so she decided to become a conductor on the underground railway. Over the next ten years she returned to the South nineteen times, and helped to free over 300 slaves,
45 including her sick and aged parents.

third person

Despite poor health, Harriet bravely devoted her life to the fight for human rights. She set up schools for ex-slaves, and homes for the sick
50 and elderly, and worked tirelessly to ensure that freed slaves could become part of society. She became known as the 'Moses of her people' because she
55 led so many to freedom.

When she died at the age of 93, Harriet was honoured by her country and given a
60 full military funeral.

Reading

1 Read the sentences about Harriet Tubman on **sheet 21**. Choose the best word, or group of words, to fit in each gap.

2 Scan Harriet Tubman's biography. Decide which details are most important and add them to the timeline of her life on **sheet 22**.

Writing

PCM 24

Write a short biography of Florence Nightingale. Use the timeline on **sheet 23** and the notes from shared writing to help you. If you wish, you could use other sources to find out more information.

REMEMBER

Features of a biography

gives facts about a person's life

based on research or interviews

includes important events

includes writer's opinions

uses past tense

uses third person

Extended Writing

Exchange your biography with a partner. Discuss possible improvements. Write a final draft of your biography.

FLORENCE NIGHTINGALE
1820–1910 An engraving of the
English nurse and hospital reformer.

DIARY
Samuel Pepys

SEPTEMBER 2nd. (Lord's Day) Some of our mayds sitting up late last night to get things ready against our feast to-day, Jane called us up about three in the morning to tell us of a great fire they saw in the City. So I rose and slipped on my night-gowne and went to her window, and thought it to be on the back-side of Marke-lane at the farthest; but I thought it far enough off; and so went to bed again and to sleep.

By and by Jane comes and tells me that she hears that above 300 houses have been burned down to-night by the fire we saw, and that it is now burning down all Fish-street, by London Bridge.

So with my heart full of trouble, I down to the water-side, and there got a boat and through bridge, and there saw a lamentable fire. Everybody endeavouring to remove their goods and flinging into the river or bringing them into lighters* that lay off; poor people staying in their houses as long as till the very fire touched them, and then running into boats, or clambering from one pair of stairs by the water-side to another.

* lighters are flat-bottomed boats

And among other things the poor pigeons, I perceive, were loth to leave their house, but hovered about the windows and balconys till they were, some of them burned their wings, and fell down.

So near the fire as we could for smoke; and all over the Thames, with one's face in the wind, you were almost burned with a shower of fire-drops.

When we could endure no more upon the water, we to a little ale-house on the Bankside, over against the Three Cranes, and there staid till it was dark almost, and saw the fire grow; and, as it grew darker, appeared more and more, and in corners and upon steeples, and between churches and houses as far as we could see up the hill of the City, in a most horrid malicious flame, not like the fine flame of an ordinary fire. We staid till, it being darkish, we saw the fire only as one entire arch of fire from this to the other side of the bridge, and in a bow up the hill for an arch of above a mile long: it made me weep to see it. The churches, houses and all on fire and flaming at once; and a horrid noise the flames made, and the cracking of houses at their ruine. So home with a sad heart.

Reading

1 What sights, sounds and smells can you find in Pepys' diary? List them on **sheet 25**.

2 a Read the impersonal account of the Great Fire of London on **sheet 26**. How does it compare with Pepys' diary extract?

b Write a short paragraph saying which account you prefer and why. Quote from the texts to support your argument.

REMEMBER

Use

note style

active verbs –
e.g. participles ('ing')

all your senses

small details

personal experience

Writing

PCM 28

Use the notes from your homework and from shared writing to draft an 'eye witness' diary entry of an important event.

Extended Writing

Write further diary entries about your imagined historical experience.

STORY WITHIN A STORY
Alexander's Story

Two children, James and the narrator, hear the sound of crying in the cellar of their boarding school. They see a small boy who tells them his name is Alexander Heracles Billings. At first they think he is one of the new boys, but then they notice that his clothes are old fashioned and there's 'something not quite right'. They realise it is the school ghost, known as 'the sad boy'. He tells them that he is sad because he is stuck there forever …

"Why are you stuck here?"

"'Cause my bones are here."

"Your b. b.. bones?"

"Yes."

5 "How come?"

And Alexander Heracles Billings took his hands away from his face and told us this story.

present tense – sense of danger

"It's 1940 and England's at war. There's bombing. The school's too close to the city so they decide to move the children to a big

10 house in the country. I don't want to go, so when everybody's milling about with labels and parents and gas-masks and packets of sandwiches, I slip away. I expect them to come searching but they don't. There are voices for a while. The sound of engines, then quiet. I'll wait till dusk, then make my way home. But at dusk,

15 I find somebody's shut the gate at the top of the steps. I call out. Yell at the top of my voice. I think they'll notice I'm not there. That they've left me behind. Somebody will come.

But nobody did, because two days later something horrible happened. The big house in the country received a direct

20 hit from a stray bomb. Most of my friends were killed, and everybody assumed I was among them. So…"

He shrugged. "Here I stayed till starvation finished me. My friends – they're all with their mums and dads now, but I can't go to mine because…"

25 "Because what?" I murmured.

"Because my bones aren't buried. They're over there, in the corner behind that great cabinet. I could show you if you like."

And he did. And then he faded out, and me and
30 James went and told Mrs Wheelright. She didn't believe a word. Marched us off to old Chocky's office. His real name's Mr Barr and he's the Head. Turned out he'd **heard** of Alexander Heracles Billings. School records.

35 So off we all go to the cellar and me and James show Chocky what's behind the cabinet and that's that.

Old Lex gets a decent burial and me and James get new nicknames. I'm Agent
40 Skull, he's Agent Moulder. I hope Alexander's having a good laugh with his mum and dad in that place where the hols go on forever.

An extract from *The Lex Files* by Robert Swindells

Reading

1 Read the text on **sheet 29**. Underline all the verbs. What tense are they?

2 Choose **three** verbs from the extract. Find one in the present tense, one in the past tense, and one in the future tense. Explain why they are in that tense.

3 Write down **three** sentences or phrases in the extract which are examples of an informal style.

Writing

PCM 31

1 Work with a partner to plan your own 'story within a story'. Use your homework notes to help you.

2 If you have time, write a few sentences together. You can write the introduction, or the beginning of the 'story within a story'.

REMEMBER

Verb tenses

Present

I walk
I am walking

Past

I walked
I was walking
I have walked
I had walked
I had been walking

Future

I will walk
I shall walk

Extended Writing

Carry on writing the story. Decide on a good title. Read your story aloud to yourself or to a partner. How can you improve it?

PARODY
Beach Party

R. L. Stine

EXTRACT ONE

She turned out the lamp on the bedtable and slid into bed.

Whatever it was in bed with her was cold, and very wet, and very slimy.

5 Karen screamed.

And struggled to get out.

But the wet slime stuck to her arms and back and the back of her neck.

She screamed again.

10 And lurched out of bed, banging her knee on the bedtable.

So slimy. So cold. All down her back. ← short sentences – sense of panic

She nearly knocked over the lamp, struggling to turn it on.

Finally the light clicked on. ←

And she saw that her bed was filled with jellyfish.

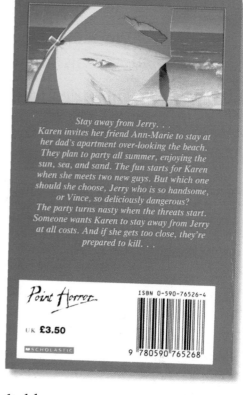

Stay away from Jerry. . .
Karen invites her friend Ann-Marie to stay at her dad's apartment over-looking the beach. They plan to party all summer, enjoying the sun, sea, and sand. The fun starts for Karen when she meets two new guys. But which one should she choose, Jerry who is so handsome, or Vince, so deliciously dangerous?
The party turns nasty when the threats start. Someone wants Karen to stay away from Jerry at all costs. And if she gets too close, they're prepared to kill. . .

Point Horror

ISBN 0-590-76526-4

UK £3.50

SCHOLASTIC

9 780590 765268

EXTRACT TWO

Vince kicked at the sand with a bony foot. Jerry moved his surfboard in front of him like a shield.

similies

They tried to stare each other down, then Vince spoke first without changing his expression.

adjectives add description

5 "Hey – you bumped me, man."

"You're a hard guy. You can take it." The slight tremble in Jerry's voice indicated that his heart wasn't entirely in this fight.

"Maybe you should stick to a boogie
10 board," Vince said, staring with distaste at Jerry's green Day-glo baggies. Vince scratched his neck. Jerry could see the tattoo on the back of his wrist, a small, black eight ball. "Maybe you should go
15 play with your *sister*," Vince said, sneering, balling his big hands into fists.

stock characters

Reading

1 Using **sheet 32** underline the typical features of popular horror used in the second extract.

2 Write brief notes about why these features are used. What effect do they have on the reader?

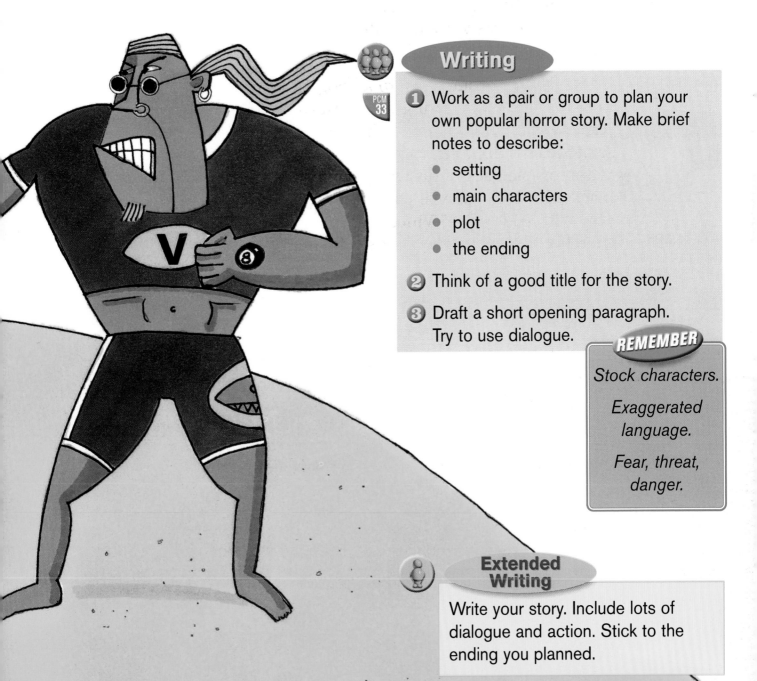

Writing

PCM 33

1 Work as a pair or group to plan your own popular horror story. Make brief notes to describe:
  • setting
  • main characters
  • plot
  • the ending

2 Think of a good title for the story.

3 Draft a short opening paragraph. Try to use dialogue.

REMEMBER

Stock characters.

Exaggerated language.

Fear, threat, danger.

Extended Writing

Write your story. Include lots of dialogue and action. Stick to the ending you planned.

What do you read

Please tick one box in answer to each question.

If none of the choices apply to you please write your own answer.

1 Are you

a girl ✓   a boy ☐

aged   5–7 years   ☐

      7–9 years   ☐

      9–11 years   ✓

      Other   ☐

2 Which type of fiction do you enjoy most?

Adventure ☐

Fairy tales, Myths and Legends ☐

Stories about animals ☐

Stories about children at home and school ✓

True stories, autobiography ☐

Science fiction ☐

Horror stories ☐

Humorous stories ☐

Other ☐

and why?

3 What makes you choose a particular book?

The picture on the cover ☐

The blurb on the back ☐

A friend says it's good ☐

The size of print in the book ☐

The author is one whose books you enjoy ☐

It is recommended by a teacher ☐

Your parent/s approve of it ☐

Other I read a bit of the story in the book

4 Where do you enjoy reading most?

At home ✓

At school ☐

Whilst travelling ☐

On holiday ☐

Other

5 Who is your favourite author?

Anne Fine

6 What is the best book you have ever read?

The Secret Garden by Frances Hodgson-Burnett

clear and simple questions

Reading

1 Choose a word from the list below and copy and complete this sentence:

> Information from the reading survey would be useful to a .... because ....
>
> ....
>
> (teacher; publisher; parent; librarian; writer)

2 Fill in the Reading Questionnaire on **sheet 34**.

Writing

Think of three more questions for the questionnaire begun in shared writing.

At least one should be multiple choice. Brainstorm all the possible answers, then choose the most suitable ones. Remember to include tick boxes next to each choice and a space for 'other' answers.

REMEMBER

What information do you want?

What questions will you ask?

How will you record the answers?

Design a clear layout.

Your questions must be simple and clear.

Extended Writing

Finish writing your questionnaire. Make a neat copy of it. You could circulate the questionnaire to another class to fill in.

Zoos

Zoos: Prisons or sanctuaries?

argues from both points of view

In 1867, a popular entertainer sang, "Walking in the zoo is the OK thing to do", but a hundred years later, this view was widely disputed. Now there is growing controversy over keeping wild animals in zoos.

states the issue

1 Cruel confinement?

MANY PEOPLE BELIEVE that depriving wild animals of their natural freedom is cruel. They see zoos as prisons, where animals suffer from stress, frustration and boredom. Other people argue, however, that wild animals are not free, even in their natural environment. They live in defined areas, where they face constant danger from hostile neighbours and humans. Far from restricting freedom, zoos provide sanctuaries in which animals can live and breed in peace.

"In every good zoo, the animal does not feel a prisoner," says Professor Hedinger of Zurich Zoo. "As in the wild, it is more like a tenant, or owner of a piece of land."

But not all zoos are good zoos, it seems. There are many complaints about standards of safety and care in both zoos and safari parks. Stephan Ormrod, of the RSPCA, says that, "Many zoo owners are ignorant of their animals' needs."

Larger zoos argue that every effort is made to meet the animals' needs: they enjoy a regular, well-balanced diet, constant shelter and are safe from predators.

2 Educational role?

ZOOS AND SAFARI PARKS are often accused of using animals for amusement and for profit. But many people insist that good zoos provide much more than entertainment. They offer a unique opportunity to learn about wildlife and visitors can study animals at close range. Opponents, however, question the educational values of zoos, where animals are seen as dependent on humans.

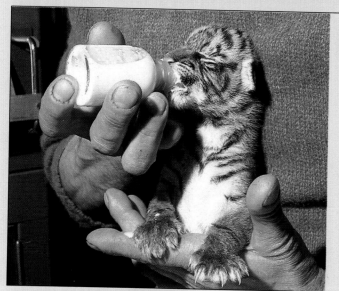

3 Saving endangered species?

MANY ANIMALS are in danger of extinction in their natural habitat, and zoos say that the animals they breed in captivity can be released back to the wild. However, critics argue that so far only five species have been saved from extinction in this way.

useful connective

(adapted from 'Zoos – prisons or sanctuaries?' from *Debates – The Use and Abuse of Animals*, by Zoe Richmond Watson)

Reading

1 Scan the report to find points for and against keeping wild animals in zoos. Record them on **sheet 35**.

2 Choose one of the phrases in the brackets. Then write out the complete sentence.

> I think zoos are (a good thing / a bad thing), because ....
> ....

Writing

PCM 37

1 Draft the second paragraph of the balanced report – arguments for. Use the notes and report plan from shared writing to help you.

2 Draft paragraph 3 of the report – the arguments against.

REMEMBER

Choose a headline.

Introduce the issue.

Give equal weight to each side of the argument.

Write your own opinion and what made you decide.

Short conclusion.

Extended Writing

Finish drafting your report. Revise it and add an introductory paragraph – your own or the one from shared writing.

ADVENTURE GAME BOOK
ISLAND OF HORROR

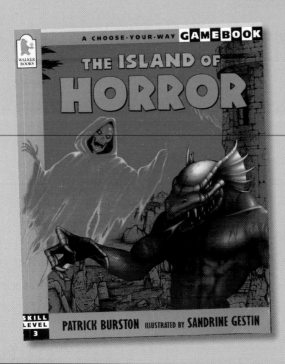

A CHOOSE-YOUR-WAY **GAMEBOOK**

WALKER BOOKS

THE ISLAND OF
HORROR

SKILL LEVEL 3

PATRICK BURSTON ILLUSTRATED BY SANDRINE GESTIN

YOUR TASK

Your plane has been shot at, and you are about to crash on a remote island. You must parachute to safety and find a way to escape. While you search, look out for the Nine Golden Skulls hidden on the island. Each Skull has a different number of teeth (from one to nine). Keep a score by copying the carving below – when you find a Skull, count the teeth and tick off that number. Keep a record of the Skulls you have found even if you are sent back to the beginning.

How many Skulls can you find before you escape?

Each time you choose a new path, you will be told which page to turn to next – but there are many dangers to be overcome and puzzles to solve. Your only friend is Rainbow the parrot. Now get ready to jump!

Good luck!

One of the skeletons has some keys which may be useful. But while you look for them, be careful where you put your feet. Suddenly Rainbow squawks to tell you you're cut off by the tide! You must swim to safety. To the headland? Or the old lighthouse?

4

If you swim out to here, turn to page 44.

If you swim to the lighthouse, turn to page 16.

19

Reading

1 Using **sheet 38** make notes and sketches for what you might see on page 44 – The headland.

Remember to include two new choices, with page numbers to turn to.

2 Using **sheet 39** make notes and sketches for what you might see on page 16 – The lighthouse.

Writing

Work in a group.

1 Using **sheet 41** quickly agree a group flowchart. This is the plan for your adventure game book: *The House of Horrors*.

2 Decide who will write and design which pages. Some people may need to do more than one.

3 Draft the text for your page. Remember to include the two new choices, but do not fill in the page numbers yet.

4 Swap texts with a partner and discuss any improvements.

5 Sketch ideas for the illustrations.

REMEMBER

Adventure game books

choice of outcomes

often in present tense

imperative verbs for instructions

plenty of action and suspense

fantasy settings and characters

include puzzles, riddles

Extended Writing

1 Continue with *The House of Horrors*. Add puzzle ideas and a scoring system as in *The Island of Horrors*.

2 Write an introduction: 'Your Task'.

16

CONVERSATION POEMS

All for an Ice Cream

All for an Ice Cream

'Mum, can I have an ice cream?'
'Go and ask your dad.'
'Dad, can I have an ice cream?'
'Go and ask your mum.'
'But I've just asked her and she told me to ask you.'
'Well tell her that I've told you to ask her.'
'Mum, Dad's just told me to tell you that you've
got to tell me if I can have an ice cream.'
'Oh well I suppose you can but go ask your dad for 10p.'
'Right.'
'Dad, can I have 10p for an ice cream?'
'I haven't got 10p.'
'Oh, come on Dad you haven't looked yet
and oh hurry, the van'll go soon.'
'Let's have a look then, ah, there you are.'
'Thanks Dad, Ohh!'
'What's the matter now?'
'The van's gone.'

Karen Jackson

Question and Answer Poem

What is the sun?
– The blushing face of the universe.
Where does the sky begin?
– Just above the smoke of the factory chimneys.
Where does nature part?
– In the middle years.
How do you cut the air?
– With the wind.
What's inside a hill?
– Things to come up in the future.
When is the end of time?
– When the last cuckoo sinks into Hell.

Written by 10-year-olds

Going Through the Old Photos

Who's that?
That's your Auntie Mabel
and that's me
under the table.

Who's that?
That's Uncle Billy.
Who's that?
Me being Silly.

Who's that
licking a lolly?
I'm not sure
but I think it's Polly.

Who's that
behind the tree?
I don't know,
I can't see.
Could be you.
Could be me.

Who's that?
Baby Joe.
Who's that?
I don't know.

Who's that standing
on his head?
Turn it round.
It's Uncle Ted.

Michael Rosen

Reading

Compare the poems *Going Through the Old Photos*, and *All for an Ice Cream*.

Working in pairs, answer these questions using **sheet 42** to help you.

1 a What is the mood of each poem?

  b What evidence of this can you find in the poems?

2 a What are the feelings of the characters?

  b What evidence of their feelings can you find in the poem?

Writing

Write your own 'question and answer' Weather Poem.

1 First, write five questions about the weather.
You could use some of the ideas from shared writing.

2 Then think of five imaginative responses. Try to use metaphors.

3 Write the first draft of your Weather Poem.

REMEMBER

Before you write, decide:

the questions

who is speaking

the mood and feelings of the poem

Extended Writing

Swap your poem with a partner. Which are the best parts? Which could be improved? Revise your work and write it out neatly for a display.

17

PUBLIC NOTICES
KEEP OFF THE GRASS!

> We reserve the right to refuse admission, alter or amend the programme as necessary. Forms for returned tickets may be obtained at the box office.

> Intermittent faults are still being experienced in some showers.
>
> We apologise for the inconvenience caused.
>
> The faults are being addressed.

THE NATIONAL TRUST
PLEASE KEEP TO THE PATHS
DO NOT CLIMB ON THE WALL
KEEP DOGS ON LEAD
KEEP THE BYELAWS

imperative verbs

KEEP OFF THE GRASS!

Do NOT PARK ON THE GREENS. IT IS ILLEGAL!!

Children under 8 must be accompanied by a swimming adult at all times.
WE THANK YOU IN ADVANCE FOR YOUR COOPERATION

polite tone

CLEAN UP
AFTER
YOUR DOG

53

CLEANING LADY WANTED

3–4 hours a week.

Good rate of pay for right person.

REFERENCES ESSENTIAL

The management cannot accept liability for accidents, loss or damage.

Reading

Work with a partner. Read the public notices on pages 52–54 and then consider these questions.

1 Where might you see these notices?

2 Who might be speaking?

3 Who is being spoken to?

4 How does the notice make you feel?

5 Might someone object to it? Why?

6 What kind of notice is it? (e.g. to do with law, safety)

Make notes of your answers.

Writing

Work with a partner to make a notice you could display in school.

1 Decide on the kind of notice you are going to write.

2 Design it carefully. Use the Remember box to help you.

REMEMBER

Notices use:

imperative verbs

passive verbs to make it impersonal

polite tone

well-designed, bold letters

typical words and phrases

Extended Writing

Continue to work on your notice, producing a final copy to be displayed around the school.

18

TANKA

Singing my Song

Singing

I'm singing my song,
The words slipping through my lips
Meet their waiting ears
Then fall into memory
To be whistled out again.

Matthew Festenstein

Tree

Swaying in the wind
I catch people's attention.
I begin to wave,
They never wave back to me.
I think nobody likes me.

Dominic Dowell

Reading

1 Practise counting syllables, using **sheet 44**.

2 Read the haiku on **sheet 45**. Change two of them into tanka. You will need to add two more lines to each haiku. Each line must have seven syllables. Try to make your lines like a reply.

REMEMBER

5 lines

syllables: 5, 7, 5, 7, 7

Say a lot in a little.

Only write about one thing.

Writing

Write your own tanka.

a Choose your subject. It is easiest to write about something you can see. Remember to write about just one thing.

b Jot down words and phrases which will make what you see and feel vivid to the reader.

c Draft the tanka. Revise and edit it until it has the correct number of syllables in each line.

Extended Writing

Swap your tanka with a partner and discuss. Is every word important? Does it sound right when you read it out loud? Make improvements. Make a neat copy of it for a class anthology.

19

NONSENSE POEMS
Bun Stew

The New Weatherperson's First Appearance

Here is the blether warcast
for Flyday the dirty-worst
of Knockedover:
    This week's cold smell
    will get curse
    towards frightfall
    with wail-force winds
    and freezing frog.
    Watch out for black lice on the toads.

Ian Serraillier

SPELLBOUND

I have a spelling chequer
It came with my PC
It plainly marks four my revue
Miss takes I cannot sea.
I've run this poem threw it
I'm shore your pleased too no;
It's letter perfect in it's weigh
My chequer tolled me sew.

Norman Vandal

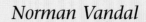

Bun Stew

Bun
Stew
I've lost my shoe
Free
Floor
Ain't got no more
Dive
Snicks
I'm in a fix
Threading
Date
I'm gonna be late
Mine
Den
Ain't seen both shoes
Since I don't know when
Elephant
Shelve
I've dug all the cupboards
So now I'll delve
Shirtbean
Shortbean
It ain't where it ought been
Fistbean
Snicksbean
Gotta be quicksbean
Threadingbean
Datebean
Time don't waitbean
Minebean
Plenty
Just have to hop
With one foot empty…

Julie Holder

Reading

1. Correct all the spelling mistakes in '**Spellbound**' using **sheet 46**.

2. **a** Write alternatives for the days of the week in the style of 'Flyday'.

   b Write nonsense alternatives for numbers up to ten in the style of '**Bun Stew**'.

Writing

PCM 48

1. Draft *either* your own Number Nonsense poem or a Whacky Weekdays poem.

2. Read your poem to your partner. Discuss possible improvements.

REMEMBER

Change letters around to change meaning.

Keep the rhyme and rhythm.

Make it absurd.

Extended Writing

Revise and edit your poem. Make a final copy to go in a class book of nonsense poems.

The Earth Centre

YOU'LL NEVER SEE **THE WORLD IN THE SAME WAY AGAIN**

Relax, explore, play and enjoy a fun day out at The Earth Centre.

400 acres of beautiful South Yorkshire landscape packed with interesting things to do and see.

imperative verbs

Experience our futuristic ideas and interactive shows both inside exciting and innovative buildings and among the inspirational gardens.

FRED SAYS:
The Earth Centre is built on the site of Cadeby Colliery which was closed in 1986 with devastating effects on the local community. In 1995 the Millennium Commission allocated a £50 million grant to Earth Centre and we started work.

Earth Centre, Denaby Main, Doncaster DN12 4EA
General enquiry number 01709 513 933
Fax 01709 512 010
e-mail info@earthcentre.org.uk

Planet Earth Experience

An immense kaleidoscopic gallery of coloured images and sounds which can transport you in a few moments from the grim roar of a busy motorway to the calm of an extraordinary rainbow created inside the building.

FRED SAYS:
After this you'll never see the world in the same way again.

Kaki Tree This is a symbol of peace. Hunt it out and discover its unique history.

FRED SAYS:
This is actually a cutting taken from a tree which survived the nuclear bombing of Nagasaki in 1945. How can we ensure peace in this new millennium?

The **Rokkaku Trail** brings all your senses to life. Be amazed by what you see, hear, feel, touch and taste. Take your shoes off and feel the textures underfoot or listen to the sounds of the sky on the huge war trumpets.

FRED SAYS:
Being bombarded with noise and fumes everyday, our senses can become dulled. We want you to experience your surroundings the way nature intended.

Inside **NatureWorks** is an exciting chance to catch creatures, examine them under a microscope or project them magnified onto a large screen and then release them into the outdoor **Wildlife Pond**.

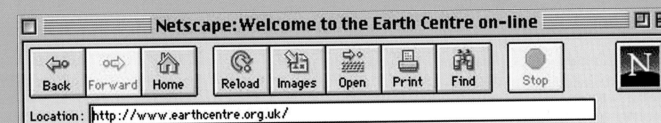

Netscape: Welcome to the Earth Centre on-line

Back | Forward | Home | Reload | Images | Open | Print | Find | Stop

Location: http://www.earthcentre.org.uk/

Live Home Page | Net Search | Apple Computer | Apple Support | Apple Software

YOU'LL NEVER SEE THE WORLD IN THE SAME WAY AGAIN

Transport Park
Ecology Park
350 acres of sky
Trans-Pennine Trail
National Cycle Network
Solar Pod
The Volcano
EarthShop
eat.organic@earthcentre
Earthonauts
Planet Earth Experience
Future Gallery
Future Child 2000
Solar Century
Earth Trail
Action News
Adventure Play Mount
Rokkaku Trail
Kaki Peace Tree
Wilderness Theatre
Forest Gardens
Dry Gardens
500 years of history
Water Works
The Living Machine
Bio Fence
Earthweb
21st Century Gardens
Yurt Project
And much, much more...

Earth centre

**Earth Centre
Denaby Main
Doncaster DN12 4EA**

**tel: 01709 513 933
fax: 01709 512 010**

**e-mail:
info@earthcentre.org.uk**

Reading

1. Read **NatureWorks** and write a typical 'Fred says' entry for it.

2. Draw a quick sketch of what you would expect to do inside **NatureWorks**.

3. Why do you think the theme park is called **The Earth Centre**?

Writing

1. With a partner, decide whether you are going to write a leaflet or web page.

2. Choose something from the list prepared in shared writing. Use this as a heading for an entry in your guide. Make a word web of things you want to say about it – facts and opinions.

3. Use the best ideas from your web to write a short, but very inviting entry. Remember who you expect to read it.

4. Revise and edit your entry. Then choose another item from the list and start to plan another entry.

REMEMBER

Decide who you are writing for.

Include facts.

Include opinions.

Be persuasive.

Invite action – use imperatives.

*Use **bold** headings.*

Extended Writing

1. Continue writing your guide. Include a full list of all the attractions: places, things, or events.

2. Design the layout carefully. Base it on a leaflet or website page you have seen.

3. Decide what illustrations you want to use and where you will put them.

PARAGRAPHS AND ENDINGS
Mountain Adventure

Butch woke up with an uneasy, unhappy feeling. He felt cold, even frightened, and didn't know why it should be.

5 He sat up, realised quickly enough where he was and why, but couldn't understand the gloom. At first he thought he must have slept through to the evening and was hurt that the others had forgotten him, and had gone home without him; he was even apprehensive
10 of walking those miles back through the rugged bush, alone, in the dark.

Then something told him he had not slept very long at all. He just didn't feel as if he had slept for hours, and the peculiar
15 popping sounds that he had been listening to were enormous raindrops hitting the rocks. The sky was black and fierce and in the distance there was the unceasing roll of angry thunder. That was why he was uneasy, and he
20 was cold because an icy wind was blustering round him.

fourth paragraph moves into action

Butch scrambled to his feet because he could see that the sky was going to split apart. He knew that when the rain really started it would
25 be a deluge and as soon as he was on his feet he remembered his blisters and his new shoes and that it was almost half a mile to the bluff where Miss Godwin and the others would be. Butch didn't know which way to run.

fifth paragraph explains how he feels

30 He'd never get to the caves. If he went on he'd be caught in the open. If he turned back he might have to scramble into the shelter of the forest. Those huge raindrops were popping more often and he could see jagged lightning
35 flashes striking between earth and cloud.

sixth paragraph – the problem gets worse

No. He couldn't go that way, because it was dangerous under the trees when the lightning struck; yet it was terrifying in the open. Each way was as bad as the other. Why
40 hadn't he hobbled on with Miss Godwin? Then he'd be cosy and safe inside the caves. Oh, why had he worn his new shoes? If only he'd changed into something old! He couldn't get
45 them on. He couldn't stand the pain. Even his toes seemed to be swollen now.

He started whimpering.

An extract from *Hill's End* by Ivan Southall

Reading

1 Choose the right words to finish each sentence.

When Butch woke up he thought ....
(he was lost / it was night-time / he had lost his shoes)

Butch knew he hadn't slept for hours when ....
(he heard raindrops / he felt an icy wind / he saw signs of a storm)

2 Using **sheet 50**, describe how Butch was feeling
at the different points in the story.

Writing

Butch is alone on the mountain.
What happens next? How will the story end?

You can use your homework notes or the notes
from shared writing to help you.

1 Make a note of the main events. Use each
event as the focus of a paragraph. Note what
Butch thinks and feels in each paragraph.

2 Write the next paragraph of the story.

REMEMBER

**Plan each
paragraph in detail**

Each paragraph should:

have one focus

link to the one before

At the end

How will Butch feel?

*How do you want the
reader to feel?*

Extended Writing

1 Continue writing the story. When
you finish, read it aloud, either to
yourself or a partner. Where do
you need to add more detail to
interest the reader? Check
spellings and punctuation.

2 Present your work neatly, in its final
form, and include illustrations.

33 Shortwood Crescent
Lydgate Green
North Yorkshire
NY8

The Manager
SAS Stores
Wellington
N8 AZY

Dear Sir/Madam

A petition of local residents will take place in the market square this coming Saturday, about SAS Stores' constant refusal to provide appropriate parking controls for customers at the Green Road store.

Customers may be attracted by your 'park-as-you-wish', approach, but seem unaware of its dangers to children, passing on their way to and from school. One child has already been hit by a car, and spent two days in hospital; there have been many other near misses.

The police have been informed of the issue and intend to monitor the situation over the next few weeks.

Yours faithfully

A Robertson

A Robertson (Mr)

St John's C of E Primary School

SEDGEFIELD WAY ◆ MEXBOROUGH ◆ DONCASTER ◆ S64 OBE

Mr Graham
West View Cottage
The Brickyards
Stamford Bridge
York
YO4 1HX

12 March

Dear Mr Graham

Thank you for taking us on a 'delightfully gruesome ghost walk'. Everyone enjoyed it very much. We thought it was really scary when you told us about the children that came back to haunt people, especially when the light in the church went out.

The other part that scared us all was when we were in the Judges' Court, and you were telling us a ghost story just when some children went by on their roller blades. The sound echoed and made us all shudder.

Thank you once again.

Yours sincerely

Jeana Cunningham

Jeana Cunningham

Hiya Trish

Hope the deadly spots have gone! It's quiet here without you! Lucky you — missing the zoo trip. It was awful. All those animals in cages like that — it's not natural. I'm going to write to the RSPCA to complain about the state of the giraffe's area. It was stinky inside and there was nothing for them to do outside. Jake was sick ha! Ha!! (Mr Benson said it was too many donuts not the giraffe smell. Uuuuugggghhh!!**!!)

Hurry back then you can help me to get up a class petition to send with the letter. I got the RSPCA address from yellow pages.

Love Claire XXXXX

Reading

Work in groups using **sheet 52**.

1 Say whether you think each sentence is true or false, and why.

2 Change the informal phrases into formal and impersonal language.

Writing

In pairs, continue working on the letter started in shared writing.

1 Think carefully about what you want to put in the second paragraph.

Each write a draft, making sure it follows on from the first paragraph.

2 Jot down ideas for the next paragraph.

REMEMBER

Formal language.

Present tense.

Extended Writing

Working on your own, finish writing your letter. Plan and write at least one more paragraph, before ending the letter formally.

Revise and edit your work. Use the opening paragraph from shared writing or write your own.

23

THEMATIC POEMS
Family Poems

Three poems by Berlie Doherty

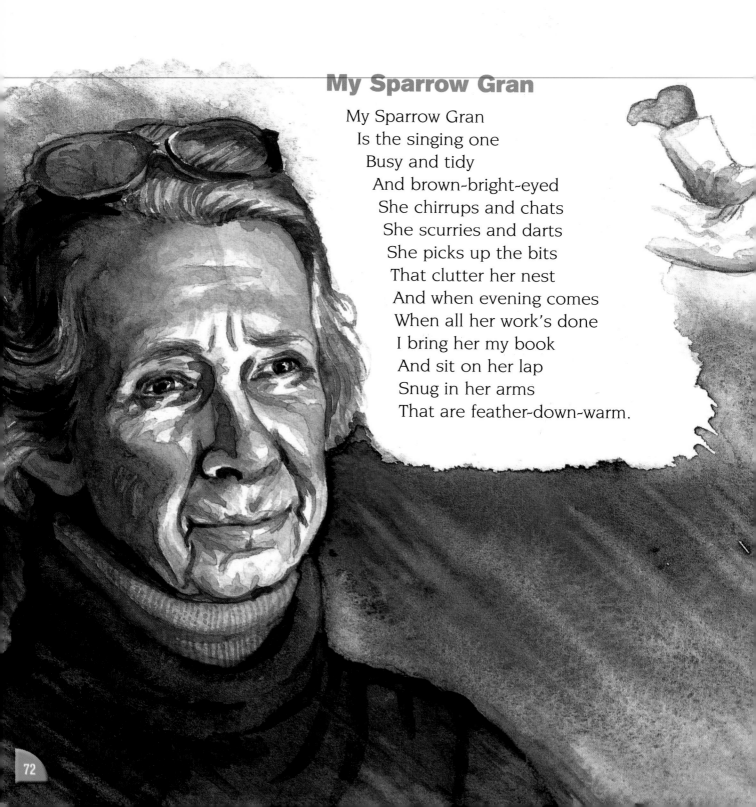

My Sparrow Gran

My Sparrow Gran
  Is the singing one
   Busy and tidy
    And brown-bright-eyed
     She chirrups and chats
      She scurries and darts
      She picks up the bits
       That clutter her nest
        And when evening comes
        When all her work's done
       I bring her my book
        And sit on her lap
        Snug in her arms
        That are feather-down-warm.

Dad

Dad is the dancing-man
The laughing-bear, the prickle-chin.
The tickle-fingers, jungle-roars
Bucking bronco, rocking-horse,
The helicopter roundabout
The beat-the-wind at swing-and-shout
Goal-post, scarey-ghost
Climbing-Jack, humpty-back.

But sometimes he's
A go-away-please!
A snorey-snarl, a sprawly slump
A yawny mouth, a sleeping lump.

And I'm a kite without a string ← metaphor
Waiting for Dad to dance again.

Grandpa

simile

Grandpa's hands are as rough as garden sacks
And as warm as pockets,
His skin is crushed paper round his eyes
Wrapping up their secrets.

73

Reading

1. Compare the three poems by Berlie Doherty using **sheet 54**.

   a How does the poet feel about each person?

   b Which words and phrases give you clues about the poet's feelings?

2. Copy and complete this sentence:

   The poem I like best is ....
   because ....

Writing

Write a poem about a person you know well, in the style of '**Grandpa**'.

1. Write a poem using a simile in lines 1 and 2, and a simile in lines 3 and 4.

2. Write a poem using a simile in lines 1 and 2, and a metaphor in lines 3 and 4.

Extended Writing

Finish your poem. Swap with a partner and discuss possible improvements. Edit and present the poem as a polished and illustrated copy to form part of your own anthology.

REMEMBER

Choose a person you know well.

Choose the best words and phrases to describe them.

Use similes.

Use metaphors.

Create mood and feeling.

24

Berlie Doherty– Talking to a poet

'I've always written poems as well as stories. A poem is a bit like a flash of lightning. It comes as a shock. Suddenly something happens that makes you want to write a poem. There's something very immediate about poetry. Obviously you can spend a lot of time afterwards reworking it, getting the right word, and polishing it. It depends on the poem. Generally the idea is there very strongly but not the form I want for it. For instance it might start off in a loose kind of shape and then develop into something more formal.

'Children sometimes try to write about abstract things. It's incredibly difficult. It's simpler to write about a particular object, describe it and what it reminds you of, what it's like, how it makes you feel. For example, recently I was walking in Belfast along the canal and I was very much moved by the beauty and peace and calm I felt in a city which has had so much strife. In the poem, 'This River Morning', I expressed the emotion through the things I saw.

'The most important thing is that a poem isn't just cut-up prose. Each line must have a vitality and music of its own. A jewel in every line. Of course sometimes you can have great fun with rhyme. It's looking at language in a new way. But you don't always have to look for a rhyme.

'If I'm writing with children I give them a starting point – like coming out in the playground and just looking about, jotting down some quick notes. Or we might start with a word, like star, or waterfall. Then we brainstorm around the words. Look at the word or phrase you like best, put a ring round it and bring it to the top, that'll be the title or the first line, or both. Then we'll look at the way we can develop from that point, describing what you're looking at and the emotion at the end so the poem builds up to that. We talk together about the words and phrases we like and why – trying to think of similes, talking about words that didn't work, finding a better way of saying it. We make sure we use all our senses – not just sight, but taste and smell and hearing and touching. Then we work on the shape of each line.'

The Wild White Horses

The day they sent
The wild white horses into the sea
Didn't they frisk, and didn't they frolic there!
Didn't they set
Their wild white manes flying
Didn't they kick their legs up high in the air!

And night and day, night and day
Don't they pound along the shore,
Don't they thunder into the sand
and pound and pound again.

Oh, set them free, set them free
The wild white horses of the sea.

Reading

Work in pairs. Read aloud the poems on **sheet 56**.

1 a What do you think each poem is about? Write brief notes, or any questions you would like to ask, around the edge of the page.

b Underline any words and phrases which you like – the 'jewels' in each line.

c Find any similes. Why do you think Berlie Doherty chose them?

2 Which is your favourite poem and why?

REMEMBER

Use all your senses.

Use similes and metaphors.

Go for a jewel in each line.

Read aloud to hear its rhythm and music.

Writing

1 On **sheet 59** write down your word and some of the descriptive words from shared writing. Add other ideas of your own. Try to think of similes or metaphors.

2 Choose your favourite word or phrase. This is the title and may be the first line.

3 Work on the first draft of your poem. Do not try to make it rhyme. Just try to find a jewel for every line. Say the poem aloud to yourself.

4 Read your first draft aloud to your partner or group. Discuss how you might improve it.

Extended Writing

Continue to work on your poem, revising and editing to produce a final polished version for an anthology.

EXPLANATION

How we Breathe

Introduction

Everybody breathes to keep
energy and blood pumping to
every part of the body, to keep
it working the way it should.
Breathing keeps us alive.

general
statement

<u>The Respiratory
System</u>

1 Air, when entering through
the nose, is filtered by hairs
inside the nostrils.

2 After it has been filtered, air
travels down the trachea
(or windpipe) and it heads
vertically to the lungs, where
there are bronchiole tubes.

3 The air goes through the
bronchiole tubes and into the
alveoli (air sacks).

Trachea

Lungs

Alveoli

bronchiole
tubes

diaphragm

This is what happens when we breathe.

air that we
breathe in
travels through
the trachea

larynx

Lungs

4 The alveoli have walls like thin
net or sheet, which are joined
to the capillaries (blood vessels).

present
tense

5 Because the walls of the alveoli are
so thin, the air bursts through
them into the blood that is in the
blood vessels.

useful
connective

6 The air is turned into oxygen and
energy by the blood cells. The
carbon-dioxide in the air is thrown
away when we breathe out.

7 Next, the blood travels to the
heart, and is pumped to all the
different organs so that they keep
working the way they should.

series
of logical
steps

David, age 11

Reading

1 Find definitions for the technical terms on **sheet 60**.

2 Take turns to tell each other how we breathe. Point to the correct part of the diagram as you explain.

3 Is there anything you can find out from the text that is not in the diagram?

4 Which box gives reasons for something happening? What does it explain?

Writing

PCM 62

1 Write an explanation of the water cycle. You can either continue the work begun in shared writing, or write your own version. Remember to look at the diagram to help you.

2 Read your finished work to a partner. Check that:

  a you have included each step

  b you have included the features of an explanation.

REMEMBER

Use connectives.

Explain how something happens and why.

Include numbered steps.

Extended Writing

Revise and polish your explanation. Make it into an information poster or leaflet.

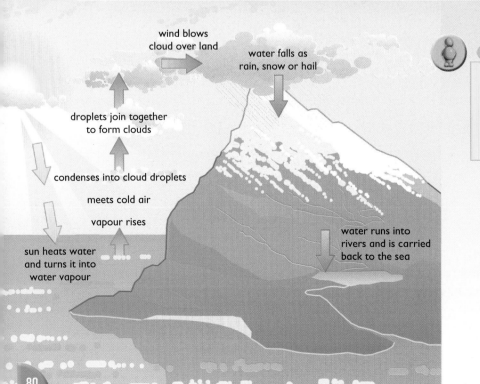

wind blows cloud over land

water falls as rain, snow or hail

droplets join together to form clouds

condenses into cloud droplets

meets cold air

vapour rises

sun heats water and turns it into water vapour

water runs into rivers and is carried back to the sea

What They DON'T tell You about . . .

ELIZABETH I
HER FRIENDS AND RELATIONS

✠ Did you know that Elizabeth I drank beer and wine for breakfast?

✠ Or that the Elizabethans washed their clothes in urine?

✠ And did you know that the nobles in Ireland entertained their guests in the nude?

If you thought that Henry VIII was a difficult monarch - think again! His tantrum-throwing daughter Elizabeth I was just as wild! Any history book will give you the boring facts THEY think you should know, but only this one will tell you what life under the world's worst-tempered queen was REALLY like...

Hodder Children's Books

U.K. £3.50 R.R.P.

ISBN 0-340-65613-1

00350

9 780340 656136

I slipped backwards and suddenly... there I was! Suspended. In mid-air.

'Help!'

From climbing and abseiling to canoeing and a Crazy Bucket Race, the adventure holiday promises to be full of action. There's just one problem as far as Tim is concerned: he is *hopeless* at sports of any kind...

Can Tim survive the horrors of a week absolutely *packed* with activity? Can his team – the Tigers – be the overall champions? There are some surprises in store for everyone!

From the award-winning author of *The Story of Tracy Beaker* and *The Suitcase Kid*.

SCHOOLS

AN ORIGINAL YEARLING PAPERBACK IN ASSOCIATION WITH CHANNEL 4 SCHOOLS

UK £3.99

ISBN 0-440-86338-4

9 780440 863380

Illustrated by Nick Sharratt

Reading

What do you think the books are about?
Write your ideas on **sheet 63**.

Writing

1. Plan a book blurb for the back cover of a favourite book. It can be fiction or non-fiction. You can use **sheet 65** (fiction) or **sheet 66** (non-fiction) to help if you wish.

2. Discuss your plan with your partner. Does it make them want to read the book? How could you improve it?

Extended Writing

Write the book blurb, using your plan. Then revise, edit and polish it. Use a word processor for the final version, or write it out carefully.

Keep a record of your 'best books' in your reading journal.

REMEMBER

Fiction blurb

use a quote from the book

summarise the plot

mention the main character

use leader dots ...

say something about the author

ask questions

Non-fiction blurb

mention the main subject

tell the reader what they can find out about ...

ask questions

use leader dots ...

E-Mail Etiquette

Subject lines

- Always include a subject line – summarising your message.
- When you reply to a message but change the subject of the conversation, change the subject line too.

The Message

- Match your message length to the type of conversation: if you are making a quick query, keep it short.

Keep to the subject

- Do not type your message in capitals – it is like shouting!
- If it is a private conversation do not worry about making corrections.

Replies

- Always respond quickly. Do not sit on e-mail for more than a few days.
- Do not rush your reply if you are angry. Re-read it when you are feeling calmer!

Signatures

- In e-mail, a signature is a little block of text at the end of your message.
- Your signature should show alternative ways of contacting you – e.g. ordinary address for letters; phone or fax number.

MESSAGES

new mail | left | right

To: forest.products@aol.com
From: jletham@demon.co.uk
Subject: Garden bench

I would like to order a three seater garden bench, catalogue number 351/021. Please take payment from my VISA credit card, number 0000 123 2344 0045 expiry date 11/02.

Please deliver to John Letham at the following address:
27 Digby Road
Manchester M14 4BT

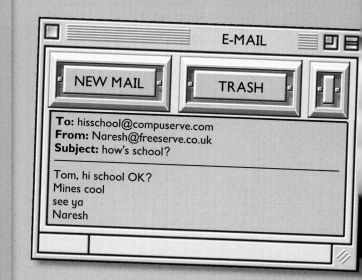

E-MAIL

NEW MAIL | TRASH

To: hisschool@compuserve.com
From: Naresh@freeserve.co.uk
Subject: how's school?

Tom, hi school OK?
Mines cool
see ya
Naresh

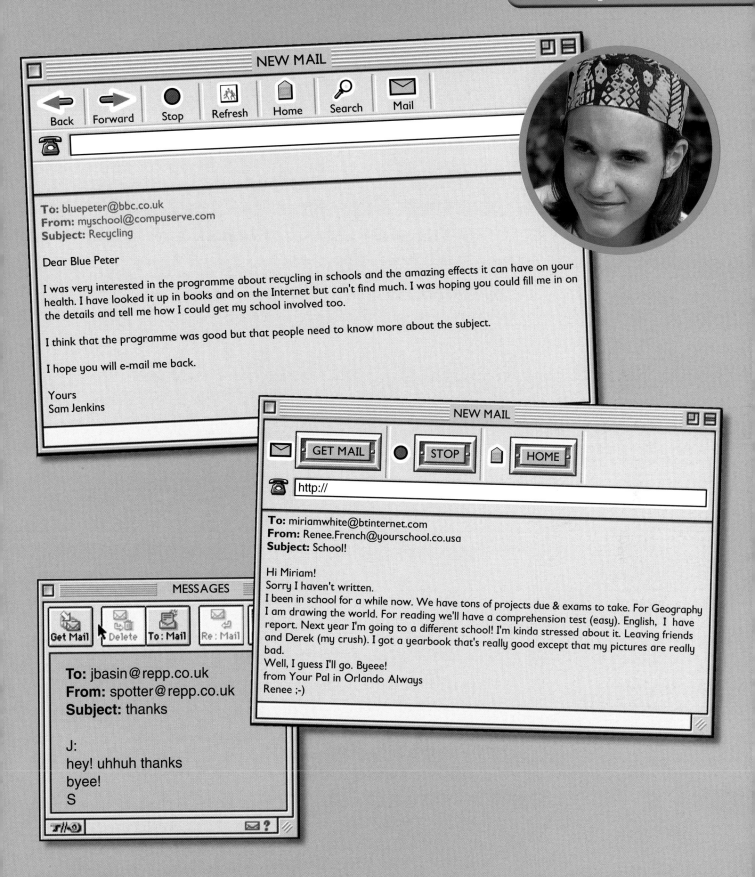

NEW MAIL

Back | Forward | Stop | Refresh | Home | Search | Mail

To: bluepeter@bbc.co.uk
From: myschool@compuserve.com
Subject: Recycling

Dear Blue Peter

I was very interested in the programme about recycling in schools and the amazing effects it can have on your health. I have looked it up in books and on the Internet but can't find much. I was hoping you could fill me in on the details and tell me how I could get my school involved too.

I think that the programme was good but that people need to know more about the subject.

I hope you will e-mail me back.

Yours
Sam Jenkins

NEW MAIL

GET MAIL | STOP | HOME

http://

To: miriamwhite@btinternet.com
From: Renee.French@yourschool.co.usa
Subject: School!

Hi Miriam!
Sorry I haven't written.
I been in school for a while now. We have tons of projects due & exams to take. For Geography I am drawing the world. For reading we'll have a comprehension test (easy). English, I have report. Next year I'm going to a different school! I'm kinda stressed about it. Leaving friends and Derek (my crush). I got a yearbook that's really good except that my pictures are really bad.
Well, I guess I'll go. Byeee!
from Your Pal in Orlando Always
Renee ;-)

MESSAGES

Get Mail | Delete | To: Mail | Re: Mail

To: jbasin@repp.co.uk
From: spotter@repp.co.uk
Subject: thanks

J:
hey! uhhuh thanks
byee!
S

New

Read

File

Delete

Search

Contacts

Check

Reading

Work in pairs.

1 Read the messages on **sheet 67**.
Which of them could be sent by e-mail?

2 a Choose one message which would be better sent by post. Explain why.

b Choose one which would be better given over the telephone. Explain why.

3 Who do you think each of these messages was sent to?

Writing

1 Using **sheet 69**, compose your own e-mail message. Use the examples in your book to help you.

2 Swap with your partner and write a reply.

REMEMBER

E-mail messages:

personal address

clear subject line

short and to the point

do not write in capitals

signature at end

respond quickly

Extended Writing

Make a list of the advantages and disadvantages of each way of sending a message on sheet 68. Write on the back of the sheet. Choose one method and write a balanced argument listing all the points for and against.

28

POETIC STYLE

Berlie Doherty– Publishing Poetry

'The editor decided on the order of the poems, and then checked with me. They are loosely ordered, a dramatic poem followed by a funny one, not in themes. Many people don't read a book of poetry from beginning to end. They pick out the titles that appeal to them, or maybe look for short ones. So I don't know whether the order really matters.

'Sometimes the editor doesn't want to include poems that you like or there are poems I don't want and the editor does. But generally we agree.

'Deciding the title of a collection is very difficult. First of all I thought of calling it after the first poem in the original collection, 'Ghost in the Garden', but it's not really typical of the other poems. 'Walking on Air' comes from a phrase in one of the poems and it sounds right, it fits the mood of the whole thing.

'Deciding which ten poems were going to be illustrated was difficult. I didn't choose them. But I did choose the illustrator. I was sent several different artists' work. I wanted a sense of fun and a magic atmosphere. Then I saw the illustrations at a very early rough stage and a couple weren't quite right so the artist changed them. The new cover is wonderful – just what I hoped for.'

A sparkling collection of poems from a prize-winning author.

Enter a world where fish swim the sky and twinkle like stars. Visit the valley of the village of secrets. Or run away with the circus school. Meet dodos, iguanas, hobgoblins and dragons. But watch out for killer plants and the terrifying Boggart.

WALKING ON AIR

BERLIE DOHERTY

ISBN 0-340-74679-3

00399

9 780340 746790

Poetry

U.K. £3.99

COVER ILLUSTRATION: **TRACEY MORGAN**

Contents

An extract from contents of *Walking on Air* by Berlie Doherty.

Reading

Work with a partner.

1 Scan the contents list of the poetry book and pick out the five poems you would read first. Discuss your reasons.

2 Look at the cover and back cover blurb.

   a What clues do they give you about the kind of poems you might find in this book?

   b Would they make you want to read this book? Give reasons.

Writing

Work as a group to make a poetry anthology.

1 Gather together all the poems you have written. Which ones do you like best and why?
Agree on which ones to include – putting in at least one from each person. Elect someone to be the editor. They have the final word!

2 Brainstorm ideas for a title. Try and find a phrase which has more than one meaning, like 'Walking on Air'.

3 Decide who will do what. You will need a cover design, a back cover blurb, a contents list, and some ideas for illustrations.

REMEMBER

Publishing a poetry collection

Which poems will you include?

Think of a title.

Plan page layout and illustrations.

Choose the order – vary the mood.

Design the cover.

Write a contents list and a persuasive blurb.

Extended Writing

Continue to work on your poetry collection. Take time and trouble to make it good enough for the library. You could use a word processor or calligraphy. You could even make your own book.

29

HOROSCOPES

In the Stars!

Aries MAR 21 – APR 20

Your stars promise fun, but there is an undercurrent running through a friendship which may get out of hand.

Taurus APR 21 – MAY 21

Expect conflicts. Co-operation is lacking and that gives rise to problems or silly disagreements.

Gemini MAY 22 – JUN 22

Your mind is dizzy with ideas and you can't get them out quickly enough. You may solve riddles.

Cancer JUN 23 – JUL 23

You can be difficult to live with. You think you are going out of your way to help, but aren't you really suiting yourself?

Leo JUL 24 – AUG 23

You're losing control of a situation and you're caught up in financial games. Be careful!

Virgo AUG 24 – SEPT 23

You think you should change your job. Your stars suggest not to plan too much. A break will come from out of the blue.

promises good news

Libra SEPT 24 – OCT 23

At times you're hard to get along with because you expect too much from others. As a Libran you want everything to balance perfectly, but other people do not have the same approach.

generalisation

Scorpio OCT 24 – NOV 22

Problems need to be addressed, particularly in the area of friendship. Sensitive issues such as money are possible starting points.

Sagittarius NOV 23 – DEC 21

It's make or break. It depends on how you are able to express yourself and be an individual. That's the crux – you cannot and must not be taken over.

Capricorn DEC 22 – JAN 20

A friendship founders on the rocks of selfishness and restlessness. If one or other of you feels trapped, then you must give your friend more space

Aquarius JAN 21 – FEB 19

Your stars point to a journey that comes upon you suddenly. Soon you'll be off somewhere which triggers a chain of unexpected events.

Pisces FEB 20 – MAR 20

Somehow you've got to let yourself go. You're not feeling yourself and are held back by someone you work or live with.

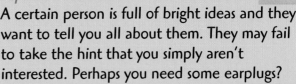

ARIES

Mar 21 - Apr 20

Today is great for any form of study. You will be able to read things and remember them. Watch out for someone who thinks they're right.

TAURUS

Apr 21 - May 21

This is the perfect day to sort out financial tangles. Sort things out properly. Avoid letting history repeat itself.

GEMINI

May 22 - Jun 22

It's easy to fall out with other people today, because no one wants to compromise. Don't burn your bridges.

CANCER

Jun 23 - Jul 23

This is a week for getting to grips with work. It's also a good chance to throw out things you no longer need.

LEO

Jul 24 - Aug 23

You can achieve so much, especially if it is creative. You also have the chance to clear up a mystery about a friend.

VIRGO

Aug 24 - Sept 23

Watch out when dealing with people in authority. Someone thinks they've got all the answers. It won't take much to rub them up the wrong way, but it will be worth the battle.

LIBRA

Sept 24 - Oct 23

A certain person is full of bright ideas and they want to tell you all about them. They may fail to take the hint that you simply aren't interested. Perhaps you need some earplugs?

SCORPIO

Oct 24 - Nov 22

If money matters have gone wrong recently, start to put them right. When dealing with a friend you need to tread a fine line between listening and letting them bully you into submission.

SAGITTARIUS

Nov 23 - Dec 21

Are you suspicious of someone? You could start to smell a rat now. However, don't leap to conclusions. Be prepared to discuss things and listen carefully.

CAPRICORN

Dec 22 - Jan 20

This is a great week for looking below the surface of things, especially if you want to get to the bottom of a mystery. Try not to get side-tracked by strange worries.

AQUARIUS

Jan 21 - Feb 19

If you are working on a future plan, this is a marvellous week for finalising things. You have a fabulous eye for detail now and this will help you sort things out.

PISCES

Feb 20 - Mar 20

It's a week for rolling your sleeves up and getting a lot of work done. Clear the air following a disagreement with a relative.

Reading

Work with a partner.

1 Each read the two versions of your own horoscope.

Do they say the same thing?

Do they conflict?

How could they fit you and your life this week?

PCM 71

2 Look at the first set of horoscopes. Write down five generalisations used.

3 Do you believe in the horoscopes? Discuss with your partner, then make notes from the text for your evidence.

Writing

Work in a group of six. Each person will write two horoscopes.

1 Decide who will write which horoscopes.

Write the first draft of one of them. Keep it short. Use the examples in your book to help you.

2 Swap horoscopes with a partner. Can you improve them?

3 Design the zodiac sign.

4 If you have time, write your second horoscope.

REMEMBER

Chatty style.

Dates in brackets.

Symbols for zodiac signs.

Generalisations.

Good news.

Dire hints.

Extended Writing

Finish writing the horoscopes. Revise them and produce illustrations. Make neat copies and paste them in place on the A3 page (**sheet 72**).

30

Writing to time

SHORT AND SWEET
Writing a story in a short time

Limit yourself to two main characters. If you have a boy and a girl it will be easy to see who's speaking – you don't have to use their names each time. (She whispered, '..., He answered, '...)

Plan the characters. Think of names. Decide one or two special details about their looks, and some traits – maybe one's impulsive and one's shy. It may be easier to base the main characters on people you know, preferably your age.

Plan a simple plot – a problem and its resolution. Somebody wants something badly – can't get it – then it's sorted out (or maybe it wasn't worth having ...). Think about how the characters change during the story.

Plan a setting – use somewhere you know so that you can make it come alive.

Get the story moving quickly. Make the opening sentences short.

Make sure the story ends on a punch line and doesn't just tail off. Think how you could link the end and beginning. ('There were so many rules in Steven's new school. He thought he'd never get used to it.' '....That was one rule Steven would never break again.') Try writing your last line before the rest of the story, so you know where you're heading!

Tell the reader what they need to know – you may know, but they can't read your mind!

Use plenty of dialogue to bring the story alive.

Use powerful verbs. ('Abby bounced/crawled out of bed' rather than 'got')

Watch out for too many 'ands' and 'thens'. Try different links. 'Several days passed...', 'Once again...', 'This time she...', 'But before he...', 'Suddenly...'.

Don't forget paragraphs.

Leave time to read the story through - at least five minutes. Check spellings and punctuation.

If you get stuck with a spelling, try out different ways on your planning sheet. Choose the one which looks right.

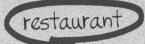

resterant   restaurant   restorant

Reading

1. With a partner, read '**The Purple Pen Story**' on **sheet 73**.

2. **a** Underline three parts you really like.

   b Underline three parts you think could be better. Make notes to say why.

3. Correct some of the mistakes – there are some speech marks and full stops missing. Look up any spellings you think might be wrong.

4. Look at the long sentence on lines 5–6. Try making it into two sentences. Use some different connectives. Does this improve the flow of the story?

Writing

Nobody was ever able to explain exactly what had happened that night.

Write a short story called 'The Unsolved Mystery'.

Ask yourself:

- What had happened?

- Who was involved?

- Why was it mysterious?

You will be working on your own.

PCM 75

1. Spend a few minutes making very brief notes on the planning sheet.

2. Start to write your story.

3. Leave five minutes to read it through. Add any extra details.

4. Check spelling and punctuation.

REMEMBER

Plan: characters (only two)

setting

problem

resolution

Use: direct speech

powerful verbs

different connectives

Get the story moving quickly.

Link beginning and ending.

End on a punch line.

Leave time to read it through and make corrections.

Extended Writing

Revise your story with help from a partner.

Acknowledgements

The publisher would like to thank the following for permission to use their copyright material.

TEXT

Unit 1: from *The True Story of the Three Little Pigs* © Jon Scieska, 1989, reproduced by permission of Viking Penguin, a division of Penguin Putnam Inc; **Unit 2**: extract from *Double Act* © Jacqueline Wilson, 1995, (Doubleday, a division of Transworld Publishers); **Unit 4**: extract one, from *Coming to England* by Floella Benjamin, reprinted by permission of Pavilion Books; **Unit 5**: 'I Met at Eve', reprinted by permission of The Literary Trustees of Walter de la Mare, and the Society of Authors as their representative; **Unit 6**: from *Beowulf* retold by Kevin Crossley-Holland (OUP, 1990); **Unit 7**: © The Independent; **Unit 11**: from 'The Lex Files' by Robert Swindells, in Just What I Always Wanted by Jacqueline Wilson et al (HarperCollins Publishers Ltd); **Unit 12**: extracts and back cover from *Beach Party* © R L Stine, 1991 (Point Horror, Scholastic); **Unit 14**: adapted from 'Zoos: Prisons or Sanctuaries' in *Debates – The use and abuse of animals* by Zoe Richmond Watson (Macdonald, 1984); **Unit 15**: from *The Island of Horror*, text © 1996 Patrick Burston, cover illustration © 1994 Sandrine Gestin. Reproduced by permission of the publisher, Walker Books Ltd; **Unit 16**: 'Going Through the Old Photos' © Michael Rosen, 1979, from *You Tell Me Poems* by Roger McGough and Michael Rosen (Kestrel, 1979); **Unit 19**: 'Bun Stew' by Julie Holder, and 'The New Weatherperson's First Appearance' by Ian Serrailier from *Crack Another Yolk*, ed. John Foster (OUP, 1990); **Unit 20**: Text and illustrations reproduced by permission of The Earth Centre; **Unit 21**: from *Hill's End* © Ivan Southall (Penguin Books, 1965); **Unit 23 and Unit 28**: seven poems, plus cover and extract from contents page from *Walking on Air* by Berlie Doherty, 1999, reproduced by permission of the publisher, Hodder and Stoughton Limited; **Unit 26**: back cover of *Cliffhanger* by Jacqueline Wilson, reproduced by permission of Transworld Publishers; back cover of *Elizabeth 1 – Her Friends and Relations* by Bob Fowke, reproduced by permission of Hodder and Stoughton Limited.

ILLUSTRATIONS

Unit 1: artwork by Carla Daly; **Unit 2**: artwork by Nick Schon; **Unit 3**: page 10, © Dan Schechter/Science Photo Library; page 11 © George Post/Science Photo Library, artwork by Gecko Ltd; **Unit 4**: artwork by Carey Bennett and Jackie Harland; **Unit 5**: artwork by Rosalind Hudson; **Unit 6**: artwork by Martin Ursell; **Unit 7**: page 22, Gamma, © Bertrand Piccard; page 23, Jellybean Photographic Services, © Brian Jones, artwork by Gecko Ltd; **Unit 8**: child picture © Penni Bickle; **Unit 9**: artwork by Rosalind Hudson; photos of Harriet Tubman, © CORBIS; Florence Nightingale photo © Custom Medical Stock/Science Photo Library; **Unit 10**: photo of painting of The Great Fire of London, by Lieve Verschuier, 1666, the Bridgeman Art Library; handmade book supplied by Rook's Book's Ltd, London, photographed by David Bradford; **Unit 11**: artwork by Joanne Moss; **Unit 12**: artwork by Julian Mosedale; **Unit 14**: page 43, Ardea, P Morris; page 44, top, Ardea, Kenneth W Fiok; page 44, bottom, NHPA © Daniel Heuchlin; page 45, NHPA © Daniel Heuclin; **Unit 15**: artwork by Ken Laidlaw; **Unit 16**: page 49 artwork by Melanie Mansfield; page 50 artwork by Rosemary Woods; page 51 artwork by Mary Claire Smith; **Unit 17**: artwork by Gecko Ltd; **Unit 18**: artwork by Nadine Faye-James; **Unit 19**: artwork by Jill Newton; **Unit 20**: photos reproduced by permission of The Earth Centre; **Unit 21**: artwork by Holly Swain; **Unit 23**: artwork by Kathryn Prewett; **Unit 24**: page 75, photo courtesy of HarperCollins publishers; page 76, artwork by Paul Dainton; **Unit 25**: artwork by Gecko Ltd; **Unit 27**: child picture © Penni Bickle; **Unit 28**: photo courtesy of HarperCollins publishers.

Every effort has been made to trace all copyright holders. The publisher would be glad to hear from any unacknowledged sources at the first opportunity.